MEXICO

GROLIER
EDUCATIONAL

Published for Grolier Educational
Sherman Turnpike, Danbury, Connecticut.
by Marshall Cavendish Editions
an imprint of Marshall Cavendish International
1 New Industrial Road, Singapore 536196

Copyright © 1997, 1999, 2001 Times Media Pte Ltd. Singapore.
Sixth Grolier Printing 2006

Set ISBN: 0-7172-9099-9
Volume ISBN: 0-7172-9110-3

Library of Congress Cataloguing-in-Publication Data
Mexico.
p.cm. -- (Fiesta!)
Includes index.
Summary: Describes the customs and beliefs connected to some of the special occasions celebrated in Mexico,
including Holy Week, Independence Day, the Day of the Dead, Saints' Days, and Huichol festivals.
Includes recipes and related activities.
ISBN 0-7172-9110-3
1. Mexico -- Social life and customs -- Juvenile literature. 2. Festivals -- Mexico -- Juvenile literature.
[1. Mexico -- Social life and customs. 2. Festivals -- Mexico. 3. Holidays -- Mexico.]
I. Grolier Educational (Firm) II. Series: Fiesta! (Danbury, Conn.)
F1210.M535 1997
394.26'0972--DC21
97-15196
CIP
AC

Marshall Cavendish Books Editorial Staff
Editorial Director: Ellen Dupont
Series Designer: Joyce Mason
Crafts devised and created by Susan Moxley
Music arrangements by Harry Boteler
Photographs by Bruce Mackie
Subeditors: Susan Janes, Judy Fovargue
Production: Craig Chubb

For this volume
Editor: Susie Dawson
Designer: Trevor Vertigan
Consultant: Chloë Sayer
Editorial Assistant: Bindu Mathur

Printed by Everbest Printing Co. Ltd

Adult supervision advised for all crafts and recipes,
particularly those involving sharp instruments and heat.

CONTENTS

MEXICO:

United States of America

Sierra Madre Occi

Culiacán

From the U.S. border two mountain ranges run south along each coast of Mexico. Between them is an enormous plateau.

Pacific Ocean

◀ **Chili peppers** make food taste hot and spicy. Most Mexican food is flavored with them.

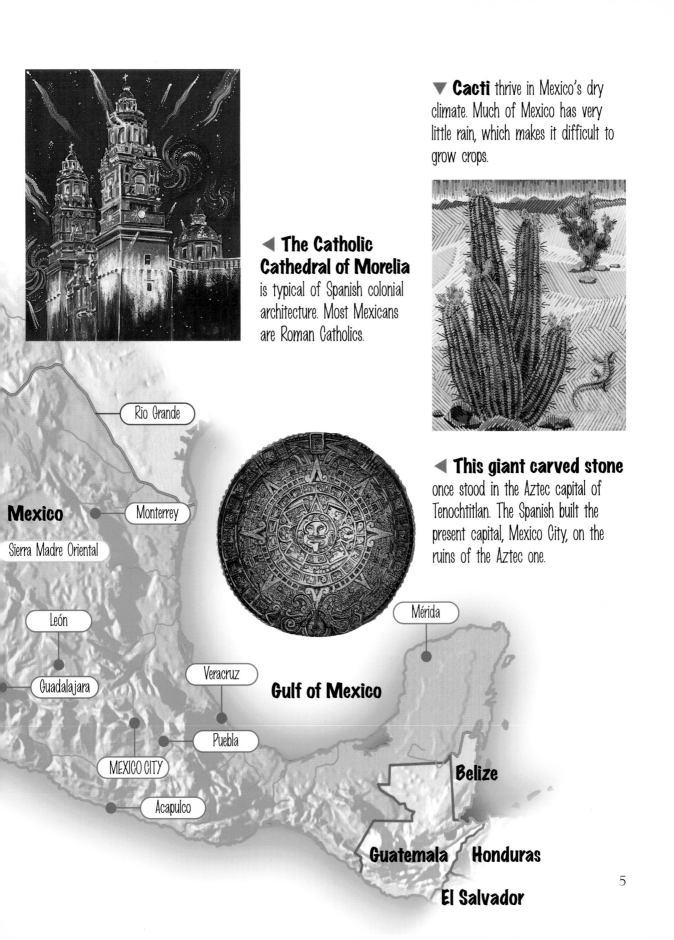

▼ **Cacti** thrive in Mexico's dry climate. Much of Mexico has very little rain, which makes it difficult to grow crops.

◄ **The Catholic Cathedral of Morelia** is typical of Spanish colonial architecture. Most Mexicans are Roman Catholics.

◄ **This giant carved stone** once stood in the Aztec capital of Tenochtitlan. The Spanish built the present capital, Mexico City, on the ruins of the Aztec one.

Rio Grande

Mexico

Sierra Madre Oriental

Monterrey

León

Guadalajara

Veracruz

Mérida

Gulf of Mexico

Puebla

MEXICO CITY

Acapulco

Belize

Guatemala   **Honduras**

El Salvador

5

RELIGIONS

Most Mexicans are Catholics. Some groups of Indians still practice their original beliefs. In many places Catholicism has been mixed with elements from these older religions.

There were many different religions in Mexico before the Spanish brought Christianity. The main thing they had in common was the belief in several gods. Of these religions the best-known is that of the Aztecs.

This figure is from a pre-Christian culture of ancient Mexico. He is holding corn cobs, a vital crop then, as now, for that region.

AZTEC RELIGION The Aztecs were very powerful when the Spanish conquered Mexico. Their gods included Huitzilopochtli, the Sun God. He needed to be fed every day with the blood from human sacrifice. Only then could he defeat the moon and stars to bring about another day. Also powerful was Quetzalcoatl, the God of Learning.

This tiny church is made of painted tin. Churches were built all over Mexico by the Spanish colonists.

CATHOLICISM is practiced by almost everyone in Mexico. It was first brought to Mexico in the 16th century by Spanish priests and missionaries. They wanted to convert all the native people to Christianity. They set about their task with enthusiasm. At first the Indians seemed to accept their teachings, but this did not last. The native people pleased their Spanish overlords by appearing to have adopted Catholicism completely, but actually they continued to use a lot of their own rituals and ceremonies. Since there were so many different groups of Indians in Mexico, today there are just as many different ways of worship in Catholicism. Each local area has its own particular ways of celebrating the major festivals. Rituals particular to one group may not be practiced anywhere else. This mixture of native and Catholic customs is still a part of Mexican Catholicism.

NATIVE RELIGION There are also some groups, such as the Huichol, who have not adopted Christianity at all. Their original beliefs have stayed virtually unchanged. There are not many of these groups, and they live in remote and often mountainous areas of the country.

This strange beast is copied from an old Aztec manuscript.

GREETINGS FROM **MEXICO!**

The people of Mexico are made up of the native peoples who first lived there and Spanish colonists who came later. Today most Mexicans have Indian and Spanish ancestors. These people are called *mestizos*. The official language of Mexico is Spanish. Mexican Spanish has adopted a lot of words from Indian languages as well as from English. There are also 56 native languages, spoken by Indian groups.

How do you say...

Hello

Hola

Goodbye

Adiós

Thank you

Gracias

Peace

Paz

7

HOLY WEEK

The week leading up to Easter, first with Palm Sunday, then with plays that reenact Christ's last few days, and finally Easter itself, are important religious holidays in Mexico.

He rode into the city of Jerusalem. In Mexico on Palm Sunday palm leaves woven into intricate shapes, including crosses, are sold at the doors of churches.

Palm Sunday is at the beginning of Holy Week. It is a time for Christians to remember the death and resurrection of Jesus Christ. During Holy Week religious people may get together to act out events from the last days of Jesus's life. These plays, called

This mask is made of goatskin and wood and is worn for Holy Week ceremonies. It is strange-looking because it represents the bad people who were responsible for Christ's death. On Saturday the mask is burned to celebrate the Resurrection.

Palm Sunday is the last Sunday before Easter in the Christian calendar. It is called Palm Sunday because on that day people waved palm leaves in the air to welcome Christ as passion plays, range from simple affairs to complicated rituals.

"Penitents" inflict pain on themselves so that they can feel some of the pain that Jesus suffered on the cross. Sometimes they tie themselves to a heavy wooden cross, which they then carry through the streets. Or they may wear a crown of thorns that makes them bleed.

Good Friday is the most important day in Holy Week, and also the most somber. It was on this day that Christ was crucified, so Friday is a day of remembrance. Statues of saints are borne through the streets, carried on the shoulders of people in the crowd. The women also carry incense, flowers, and candles. Easter hymns are sung by all.

A papier-mâché figure of the devil sticks his tongue out mockingly. Figures like this represent Judas and are bought during Holy Week. The small head of a devil is a toy rattle bought for children.

On the following day, Saturday, figures of Judas are burned. Judas was a disciple of Jesus. He was tempted by the devil to betray Jesus, so he is portrayed as a devil figure. Papier-mâché figures of this character are sold. Sometimes the devil's head is replaced by the head of a hated figure. During World War II Adolf Hitler was a popular choice.

The figures used to be wrapped in fire-crackers. When they were lighted, they broke up in a shower of sparks. Today they are just burned. Destroying them by setting them on fire represents the victory of the forces of good over evil, just as Christ triumphed by rising from the dead.

INDEPENDENCE DAY

Mexico gained independence from Spain in 1821. Since then this event has been celebrated each year on September 16.

The festivities for this great event in Mexican history begin on the night of September 15. In every town and village square throughout the country people gather to reenact the events of almost 200 years ago, when Mexicans first attempted to free themselves from Spanish rule.

LA CUCARACHA

Ya mur-ió la cu-ca-ra-cha, Ya la lle-van a-en-te-rrar en-tre cua-tro zo-pi-lo-tes y un-ra-tón de sa-cris-tán. La cu-ca-ra-cha, la cu-ca-ra-cha, ya no pue-de ca-mi-nar Por-que le fal-ta, por-que no tie-ne, u-na pa-ta para an-dar

The poor cockroach is dead
and is going to be buried
by four big vultures,
and an undertaker mouse.
The cockroach, the cockroach,
Poor thing cannot walk,
What she needs, what she
is missing,
Is another leg to walk.

the steps or balcony of the Town Hall, cries "Viva Mexico! Viva la independencia!" meaning "Long Live Mexico! Long Live Independence!" The waiting crowd takes up the words and roars them back.

These events are played out every year in memory of the rousing call made by Father Hidalgo on the same day in 1810. He urged his fellow Mexicans to fight for independence. But it took eleven years from that date for the Mexican people to finally overthrow their Spanish rulers.

The celebrations end with a display of fireworks.

People crowd into the squares, blowing papier-mâché horns and waving Mexican flags. Children throw handfuls of red, white, and green confetti. They also break flour-filled eggshells over the heads of friends or strangers.

At 11 p.m. a local official, standing on

An Independence Day banner shows the bell rung by Hidalgo in 1810 as well as the words he shouted.

The sombrero has become a symbol of Mexico. This silver-embroidered sombrero is for special occasions. Wide-brimmed hats were worn for protection against the sun.

DAYS OF THE DEAD

Mexicans believe that the dead return to visit the living between October 31 and November 2. The dead souls can even taste their favorite food.

All Saints' Day, on November 1, and All Souls' Day, on November 2, are days recognized by all Christian countries.

It is in Mexico alone, however, that these days have taken on a huge significance. The rituals associated with these days are a mixture of Catholic and native beliefs. Death is seen as part of life in Mexico. The dead are never forgotten, and people believe the dead return for a few days each year to be with the living.

Celebrations vary from region to region. Altars for returning souls are set up in a corner of the home.

Made from wire and papier-mâché, a skeleton delivery boy races through the streets with newspapers piled unsteadily behind him.

Some have frames decorated with yellow and orange marigold flowers. These are symbols of the short time humans spend on earth. Offerings to the dead are laid out on the altars. They may include fruit, special bread, sugar skulls, paper cutouts, candles, and photos of the dead. Favorite foods and drinks of the dead souls are included.

SKELETON PUPPETS

1 Cut skeleton shapes out of colored cardboard. Punch holes for fasteners. Put the skeleton together with right arm in front and left arm behind. Decorate the skeleton and the guitar.

2 Fasten on the guitar. Make a a hole in the top of each leg and in the top of the left arm. Take two pieces of string. With the two legs crossed, thread one piece of string between the two leg holes. Tie, with length dangling.

3 Thread the other string through hole in the top of the left arm. Tie it on, with a length dangling. With legs crossed and arm in downward position, tie the dangling piece to the leg string. Tape a stick to the back.

YOU WILL NEED
Thin colored cardboard
Paper fasteners
String
Thin sticks

MEXICAN HOT CHOCOLATE

Hot chocolate is a favorite Mexican drink. This is why it is often placed on altars for Days of the Dead. The stick on the right is a Mexican utensil for whisking hot chocolate. *Masa harina* is sold in Tex-Mex stores.

MAKES 12 CUPS

1 cup masa harina
(Mexican corn flour)
1½ quarts water
2 tbsp ground cinnamon
6 squares unsweetened
chocolate, grated
About 2 cups packed
brown sugar
1½ quarts milk

Cacao beans are crushed on a typical Mexican grinding stone. Chocolate and cocoa are made from cacao beans.

1 Sift masa harina into a large saucepan. Make a well in the middle. Gradually stir in water, until smooth. Stir in cinnamon.
2 Put pan over low heat, and simmer, stirring constantly, until thickened.
3 Add chocolate, 2 cups sugar, and milk. Stir until chocolate and sugar are dissolved. Taste, and stir in extra sugar if it isn't sweet enough.
4 Use an electric mixer to beat until frothy. Ladle into mugs, and serve while still hot.

October 31 is the day when the souls of dead children return to earth. They are known as the *angelitos,* or little angels. Toys and candies are placed on the altar for them.

The following day is the turn of the adult souls. The church bells ring to welcome them home. Paths of petals are sometimes laid out from the cemetery to the house to make sure the souls of the dead do not lose their way. As with the angelitos, the favorite foods of dead adults are laid

Real fruit and vegetables are left on the altars for the dead to enjoy. These are papier-mâché models.

out. Children may go from house to house asking for gifts. They receive gifts of money.

On the morning of November 2 everyone goes to the cemetery to say a last farewell to the departing souls. They take flowers, candles, and incense. Then they say good-bye until next year, when the dead will be sure to return again.

Sugar skulls are sometimes put on altars for the dead. More often they are given as a joke to the living. The name usually belongs to the person to whom the skull is given.

These papier-mâché skeletons are certainly enjoying the festivities.

15

JUAN THE NONBELIEVER

Mexicans believe that during the Days of the Dead, the souls of dead relatives come back to earth for a brief visit. They set up elaborate altars piled high with offerings for them to enjoy. It may surprise some people how much trouble and expense Mexicans go to for this occasion. The following story helps to explain why.

IN A SMALL Mexican village there lived a newly married couple. When the Day of the Dead was approaching, the wife asked her husband for some extra money. She wanted to prepare an offering for his dead parents.

"What a load of nonsense!" he said. "I'm not wasting my hard-earned money on ridiculous superstitions." His wife was rather shocked at his response and pleaded with him.

"Your parents will feel sad and neglected if we do not provide them with anything."

"If you really feel so strongly about it, then find some old thing to offer them. It hardly matters what." With that he stormed off to work.

The young wife did the best she could. She set up an altar and spread it with a ragged cloth. All she could find as offerings were water in an old cup and an apple. She and her husband were poor and did not have much to spare.

Later that evening her husband was on his way home from work when he saw a procession of people walking toward the cemetery. Most of them were carrying heavy loads. They were laden down with baskets of fruit,

cooked food, flowers, and candles. At the back, however, were an old couple carrying nothing but a cracked cup and an apple. Whereas the main group were happy and had smiling faces, the two at the back seemed gloomy and sad. On closer inspection he recognized the two people at the back — they were his own parents. Trembling with shock and fear, he ran home and asked his wife.

"Did you set up an altar with a cracked cup and an apple on it?"

"Yes," she answered. "I knew that your parents would return and that they would think we had forgotten them altogether if we left nothing."

Her husband told her what he had seen and how terrible he felt. He vowed never to be so cheap again. From then on they always left a huge pile of offerings for his parents to enjoy.

OUR LADY OF GUADALUPE

For a few days in the middle of December the whole of Mexico pays tribute to its patron saint, the Virgin of Guadalupe.

The image of the Virgin of Guadalupe appears everywhere. Here it is printed as an embroidery pattern. Across the top is written "Queen of Mexico."

No other figure to do with Christianity is more loved throughout Mexico than the Virgin of Guadalupe. Statues and pictures of her are displayed in every home. On December 12 of each year Mexicans show their devotion in a vast display of public adoration.

A week or more of preparations leads up to the big day, when children go to church dresssed in Indian costume. The girls wear brightly colored necklaces, shawls, and embroidered blouses. The boys wear *sarapes* (the Mexican poncho) and sandals, and have painted-on mustaches. These boys are called *Dieguitos* in memory of an Indian called Juan Diego, who saw the Virgin Mary in a miraculous vision.

A big celebration takes place in Mexico City at the Basilica de Guadalupe. It was here on December 12, 1531, that the Virgin first appeared to Juan

This highly ornamented Christian cross is bought by Mexicans to hang in their homes. It has pictures of saints and is dotted with good luck charms.

Diego as a dark-haired, brown-skinned woman. The Virgin demanded that a church be built on the site. To persuade Juan Diego she was real, she made roses bloom on the barren hillside.

Many Mexicans believe images of the Virgin of Guadalupe have caused miracles. She is supposed to have healed hundreds of sick people.

The Virgin's wish was granted. There are two churches on the site today. On December 12 the area is packed with joyous Mexicans. Groups of dancers from far-off towns and villages perform in her honor. People throng into the church to pay homage to her image.

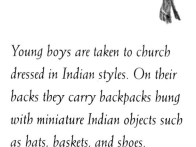

Young boys are taken to church dressed in Indian styles. On their backs they carry backpacks hung with miniature Indian objects such as hats, baskets, and shoes.

CHRISTMAS

As in all Christian countries, Christmas is a time of great celebration. It begins nine days before December 25 and continues until January 6.

The poinsettia is known in Mexico as the Christmas flower, partly because of its red color and partly because it blooms mainly in December. It is named after a U.S. ambassador to Mexico, Joel R. Poinsett. He liked the flower so much that he named it and sent it to the United States and Europe.

Markets become full of model *nacimientos*, or nativity scenes, as Christmas draws near. The figures are usually made of clay and then painted. The ones shown above were made in this way. Nacimientos used to be the most important Christmas decorations, but they are slowly being replaced by Christmas trees, as influence from the United States becomes more widespread.

In the nine days before Christmas Day itself *posadas* are held in memory of Mary and Joseph's journey from Nazareth to Bethlehem and their search for a place to sleep every night. Children and adults visit neighbors and ask for posada or shelter, as Mary and Joseph did so long ago. They go from house to house in procession, carrying candles and singing carols along the way. At the end of their journey they break open a *piñata* and hungrily eat the candy inside.

MAKE A PIÑATA

A *piñata* is a toy that is made for festive occasions, particularly Christmas or birthdays. It is made of papier-mâché and is hollow. It can be any shape: animals and cartoon characters are both popular. It is filled with candies, fruit, nuts, and small toys, and hung from the ceiling. Everyone sings a song while a blindfolded child tries to break the piñata with a stick. When it does eventually break, everyone rushes to get the contents which have fallen to the ground.

YOU WILL NEED

Newspaper • Balloon
Wallpaper paste
Thick paper • String
Poster paints • White glue
Colored tissue paper

1 Blow up a balloon. Cover the balloon with strips of newspaper covered with wall-paper paste. Leave to dry. Tie strong string around the balloon and glue in position. This string will be used to hang up the piñata. Make seven cone shapes from quarter-circles of thick paper.

2 Cut slits in the cone edges. Tape the cones onto the balloon, then cover the whole shape with more newspaper and paste. Leave to dry. Carefully cut a hole at the top of the shape, avoiding the string.

3 Paint your piñata with poster paints. For a glossy finish, varnish it with diluted white glue. Make tassels of tissue paper. Snip ends of cones and insert the tassels. Fill the piñata with candy.

21

Pastorelas are held at the same time. These are short plays in which the events leading up to Christ's birth are acted out.

Presents are not brought to children until January 6, the feast of Epiphany or the Three Kings. This is in memory of the gifts of gold, frankincense, and myrrh given to baby Jesus in Nazareth by the Three Kings.

There is also a special Epiphany supper of a ring-shaped cake and a drink of hot chocolate. A tiny plastic baby is hidden inside

This paper cutout is a Christmas decoration. At the top is written "Feliz Navidad" or Merry Christmas. It shows a piñata being broken.

PIÑATA BREAKING SONG

An - da - le, Pe - pe, no pier - das el ti - no —

— Que de la dis - tan - cia se pier - de el - cami - no.

Con los o - ji - tos ven - da - dos y en las ma - nos un bas - tón. —

Se ha - ce la olli - ta peda - zos sin te - ner le com - pa - sión da - le, da - le,

da - le, no pier - das el ti - no, Que de la dis - tan - cia se pierde el ca - mi - no.

Come on Pepe, don't lose your touch,
Your aim from a distance misses the piñata.
With your eyes blindfolded and a stick in your hands,
Break the jar to pieces without compassion.
Hit it, hit it, hit it, don't lose your touch,
Your aim from a distance misses the piñata.

the cake. Whoever gets the slice that contains the baby is obliged to give a *tamales* party to all those present on February 2, which is Candlemas Day.

Tamales are a traditional Mexican food. They are often made for festivals. The part you can eat is made of corn dough with a meat or poultry filling. The dough is then wrapped in dried corn husks or banana leaves and steamed. Many members of the family gather together to make them. This ensures that preparing them is just as much fun as eating them.

ZUCCHINI AND CORN

SERVES 4

2 tbsp butter or margarine

1 large onion, chopped

1 green bell pepper, cored, seeded, and chopped

1½ pounds zucchini, sliced

2 cups frozen whole-kernel corn

2 tomatoes, chopped

4 tbsp water

Salt and pepper

1 Heat oven to 350°F.
2 Melt butter or margarine in Dutch oven over medium heat. Add onion and bell pepper and cook 5 to 7 minutes, stirring until soft. Add zucchini. Stir until coated with butter or margarine.
3 Turn off heat. Add corn kernels, tomatoes, and water to Dutch oven. Add salt and pepper. Using a long-handled wooden spoon, stir together. Cover Dutch oven.
4 Put Dutch oven in oven, and cook for 20 minutes.
5 Wearing oven mitts, remove Dutch oven from oven, and place on stovetop. Remove lid.
6 Use tip of knife to pierce pieces of zucchini to test that they are tender. If they are not, re-cover Dutch oven, and return it to oven for 5 minutes longer. Be careful because it will be hot!
7 Taste and add salt and pepper to taste.
8 Spoon zucchini and corn mixture into a serving bowl. Serve at once, while still hot.

Corn is a very common food in Mexico. It is eaten whole as here or ground into flour and made into other dishes.

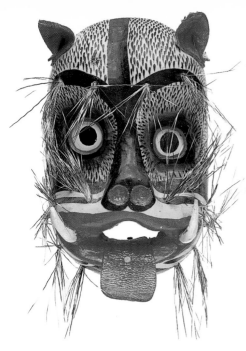

SAINTS' DAYS

Local saints all have their own particular day that is celebrated annually in the village or town to which they belong. The festivities include processions, dances, and food, and end with huge fireworks displays.

Each village or town has its own patron saint. The day of the saint's birthday gives the whole community a chance to forget its daily worries and join together in the excitement of celebration.

The main feature of the day is the procession of the saint's statue through the streets. Dancers and musicians lead the procession. Some dancers wear masks. These often represent animals, like the tiger mask shown above. People line the streets to watch, and stands sell corn-on-the-cob and cotton candy.

The fiesta always ends with a dramatic fireworks display. The fireworks are built on structures made of bamboo. One of these is known as the *castillo,* or castle; another is called the *torito,* or little bull. The torito has horns and is carried on a man's shoulders. The man then runs around like a bull chasing people while the fireworks explode all around his head. This is very dangerous!

Dancers and musicians gather outside the church for a local festival. The picture is painted on bark paper.

MILAGROS

These small offerings are known as *milagros* or miracles. They are pinned to the robes of saints' statues in churches. They are offered either when help is being asked for or as thanks for help received. The shape of the *milagro* relates to the kind of help required. For example, an eye is for a cure to that part of the body, or a donkey is for an illness affecting the person's donkey.

This drum and pipe are typical of the kind of instruments played on the streets at festival times.

25

THE CONQUEST OF MEXICO

In 1519 the Spaniard Cortés and his men marched to the Aztec

capital of Tenochtitlan and defeated the Aztec empire.

Special dances are held in which people reenact that defeat.

IT WAS ON August 16, 1519, that Hernan Cortés and his band of 400 men set off from the coast of Mexico to conquer the mighty kingdom of the Aztecs, who ruled over much of Mexico at that time. The Spanish wanted Mexico for themselves.

As they came over a high pass, they saw the Aztec capital before them. Tenochtitlan was a beautiful city. The Aztec ruler, Montezuma, awaited them. Montezuma had heard about the arrival of the Spanish and believed that Cortés must be the god Quetzalcoatl returning to his people. According to Aztec legend, the returning god would arrive from the sea, as Cortés had.

On November 8 the Spaniards marched into the city. When Cortés and Montezuma met, Montezuma welcomed Cortés like a god. But Cortés abused the king's kindness — he kidnapped Montezuma and held him hostage. Some time later there was a misunderstanding between the Spanish and the Aztecs, and the Spanish killed hundreds of Aztecs. The angry Aztecs then attacked the Spanish. To try to calm the Aztecs, Cortés made Montezuma plead for peace. As the emperor spoke, he was hit by a stone on the head and killed.

Convinced that the Spanish had murdered their emperor, the Aztecs attacked more fiercely. After a terrible battle and with the help of other Indians, Cortés eventually defeated the Aztecs. He destroyed the Aztec capital and made the proud Aztecs his slaves.

HUICHOL FESTIVALS

The Huichol Indians live in a mountainous part of western Mexico. Their religious beliefs have changed very little since the arrival of Christianity.

The gods of the Huichol Indians include Father Sun, Grandfather Fire, and also Grandmother Growth. Together they provide most of the necessities of life. The Huichol Indians ask them for protection and blessings.

The Huichol year is dotted with festivals and ceremonies. Most of them celebrate the crops and the harvest. The Feast of the Ripe Fruits is the time when the Huichol give thanks for the new harvest of corn, their main crop.

The Huichol spend a lot of time preparing offerings for the gods, including beautiful bowls lined with beads, pictures made of yarn, arrows decorated with tiny objects, and "gods' eyes" made of yarn wound around two small sticks.

This picture is made with strands of yarn laid over a base of warm wax. The design contains many Huichol religious symbols.

GODS' EYES

The Huichol believe that their gods can keep watch over them by means of "gods' eyes." These gods' eyes are made of strands of brightly colored yarn stretched onto wooden crosses. They are made as offerings to the gods and left for them in caves and other sacred places. Huichol children wear them for the Feast of the Ripe Fruits.

1 Tie two popsicle sticks together with a strand of colored yarn and knot the yarn at one end.

2 Start winding the yarn around the middle of the cross, going over and under each stick in turn.

3 To change color, knot the end of the first piece of yarn to the beginning of the second. Cut off any long loose ends.

4 Leave room for tassels on the ends of the sticks. To make the tassels, wind a length of yarn around two fingers ten times.

YOU WILL NEED

Popsicle sticks or thin lengths of wood
Colored yarn
Scissors

5 Attach the tassel to end of one stick by winding some yarn around it. Repeat for all stick ends. Snip three of the tassels, leaving one to hang up the god's eye.

29

MASKED DANCES

Masked dancing is at the heart of every Mexican fiesta. Its roots lie far back in ancient times.

Before the arrival of the Spanish Mexicans used a variety of masks in their religious ceremonies. Priests wore masks that were made to look like the gods. Dancers wore masks of the animals the people wished to hunt and kill to protect their crops.

Later the Spanish introduced Christian themes into the dances, and new masks with fair skin, beards, and blue eyes were made.

Devils were another popular subject.

Masked dancing is still performed at Mexican ceremonies. Dancers take their roles seriously and rehearse beforehand. They are performing a religious duty for the community.

Masks are made of wood, cloth, leather, clay, tin, and paper. They are sometimes made with real hair and teeth.

One of the most common dances centers on the tiger. It is performed to ensure a good crop in the year to come. The dancer wears a tiger mask and a striped or spotted costume. In the dance the tiger pretends to damage the crops. Angry farmers then chase him away.

WORDS TO KNOW

Altar: A table on which worshipers leave offerings, burn incense, or perform ceremonies.

Aztecs: A Mexican people who founded an empire and were conquered by the Spanish in 1519.

Candlemas: A festival commemorating the visit of Mary and Jesus to the Temple in Jerusalem. Catholics celebrate this day by lighting candles.

Colonist: A settler. Colonists live in lands ruled by the countries that they or their families come from. These lands are called colonies.

Incense: A mixture of gum and spice that gives off a pleasing smell when burned. Incense is often used in religious services.

Mestizo: A person of mixed Spanish and Indian ancestry.

Missionary: A person who is on a mission to convert others to a particular religion. Missionaries are usually Christian or Muslim.

Passion play: A play that tells the story of the Passion – the sufferings of Jesus Christ between the Last Supper on Maundy Thursday and His crucifixion on Good Friday.

Patron saint: A saint who watches over a particular group. Nations, towns, and professions all have patron saints.

Resurrection: The rising of Christ from the dead on Easter Sunday.

Roman Catholic: A member of the Roman Catholic Church, the largest branch of Christianity. The head of this Church is the pope.

Saint: A title given to very holy people by some Christian churches. Saints are important in the Roman Catholic Church.

Sombrero: A tall, wide-brimmed hat.

Soul: Christians believe that people have souls which leave their bodies when they die.

ACKNOWLEDGMENTS

WITH THANKS TO:

Juliet Martinez and Marcela Leos, Cultural Section, Embassy of Mexico, London. Mexicolore, London. Yolanda Paez, Mexico. Si Señor Mexican Restaurant, London. So High Soho craft shop, London. Tumi Ltd., Importers of Latin American Crafts, Bath and London.

PHOTOGRAPHS BY:

All photographs by Bruce Mackie except: David Lavender p8(right), p18(right), p24(right), p25(top), p28(top), p30. Cover photograph KL Benser/ZEFA.

ILLUSTRATIONS BY:

Fiona Saunders title page p4-5, Mountain High Maps ® Copyright © 1993 Digital Wisdom, Inc. p4-5. Tracy Rich p7. Robert Shadbolt p17. Tony Smith p27.

SET CONTENTS